Need to Know
ADHD

Philippa Pigache

www.heinemann.co.uk/library

Visit our website to find out more information about **Heinemann Library** books.

To order:

 Phone 44 (0) 1865 888066

 Send a fax to 44 (0) 1865 314091

 Visit the Heinemann Bookshop at www.heinemann.co.uk/library to browse our catalogue and order online.

Produced by Monkey Puzzle Media Ltd
Gissing's Farm, Fressingfield, Suffolk IP21 5SH, UK

First published in Great Britain by Heinemann Library, Halley Court, Jordan Hill, Oxford OX2 8EJ, part of Harcourt Education.
Heinemann is a registered trademark of Harcourt Education Ltd.

Editorial: Clare Collinson
Design: Jane Hawkins
Picture Research: Sally Cole
Consultant: Andrea Bilbow, ADDISS
Production: Viv Hichens

Originated by Ambassador Litho Ltd
Printed and bound in Hong Kong, China by
  South China Printing Company

ISBN 0 431 18840 8 (hardback)
08 07 06 05 04
10 9 8 7 6 5 4 3 2 1

ISBN 0 431 18847 5 (paperback)
09 08 07 06 05
10 9 8 7 6 5 4 3 2 1

British Library Cataloguing in Publication Data
Pigache, Philippa
  ADHD. – (Need to know)
  1.Attention-deficit hyperactivity disorder – Juvenile literature
  I.Title
  616.8'589

Acknowledgements
The publishers would like to thank the following for permission to reproduce photographs: ADD Consults p. 20; AKG-Images pp. 8, 9; Alamy pp. 14 (David Young-Wolff), 17 (Jackson Smith), 25 (David Young-Wolff), 26 (David Freeman/Fog Stock), 36 (Margaret Mitchell), 42–43 (Plain Picture/S. Kuttig); Corbis pp. 4–5 (Jon Feingersh), 6 (Norbert Schaefer), 13 (Patrik Giardino), 19 left (Franco Vogt), 21 (LWA-Dann Tardif), 35 (Francisco Villaflor), 37 (ER Productions), 44–45 (Lynda Richardson), 46 (LWA-Dann Tardif), 49 (Bettmann), 51 (Mug Shots); Mark Henley p. 11; MPM Images p. 31; Photofusion p. 7 (D. Christells); Rex Features pp. 1 (SIPA), 19 right (Affinity), 23 (Saukkomaa/LHT), 29 (SIPA); Science Photo Library pp. 24 (BSIP V&L), 27 (Dept. of Nuclear Medicine, Charing Cross Hospital), 28 (Alfred Pasieka), 30 (Jim Varney), 32 (James King-Holmes), 41 (Tracey Dominey), 40 (R. Maisonneuve/Publiphoto Diffusion), 47 (Hattie Young); Topham Picturepoint p. 38 (A Thurlby/Syracuse Newspapers/Image Works).

Cover photographs reproduced with permission of Rex Features (SIPA) and Corbis (Franco Vogt).

Contents

Any words appearing in the text in bold, **like this**, are explained in the Glossary.

Introducing ADHD

ADHD stands for Attention Deficit Hyperactivity Disorder. Yes, it's a mouthful. This is because it is an illness defined by symptoms: in this case, things people do. People with ADHD don't have spots, a nasty cough, a bad colour or a funny expression. They look just like other people. In fact in nearly every way they are just like other people. But a small difference in the way their brains work causes them to behave in a special way that can make their lives and those of their families and friends very difficult.

Not all people with ADHD have the same symptoms, but all of them have one or more of the following problems:
- they have difficulty paying attention
- they cannot focus on just one thing at a time
- they find it almost impossible to sit still
- they do things without considering the consequences
- they lose things, forget things and can't keep track of what they're supposed to do.

ADHD is a condition that chiefly affects children. It affects adults too, but the damage it does to children's lives can be much greater because it has a knock-on effect on their families, friends, classmates and teachers. It can prevent children from making friends, it can get them into trouble, make them unable to finish their homework, break up their families, and turn their classrooms into chaos.

As doctors get better at recognizing the signs and symptoms of the condition, more people – grown-ups as well as children – are being **diagnosed** with ADHD, and more people are receiving treatment. Experts believe that at least three children in every hundred between the ages of four and fourteen, and possibly many more, may have ADHD. Not all of them are seen by doctors of course. In countries where there are so few doctors that even life-threatening diseases go untreated, no one keeps a record of who may have ADHD. But research that has been carried out in many countries leads us to believe that the same proportion of children have ADHD whether they are in Hong Kong or Honolulu, Australia or Africa.

Mental illness

It's not difficult to recognize that a person is ill if there are clear, physical signs of illness. If they have a pain, or an infection that produces a fever, or they eat something that makes them feel sick and throw up, people feel sympathetic and want to help. But if something goes wrong in a person's brain, the control-centre of the body, they are not so obviously 'ill'.

Nevertheless, a small 'blip' in the way the brain functions can cause mental illness that can make a person unhappy, odd or difficult to deal with. Instead of offering sympathy, people may say things like: 'Pull yourself together!', 'You've got no self-discipline,' 'His parents can't cope,' or 'She's just going through a stage.' They do not realize that he or she may not be able to control their behaviour.

Children with ADHD may find it impossible to concentrate long enough for even simple board games.

❝He was charging around the house waving this plastic machine-gun like a loony. He swept all the plants off the window sill and broke the lot.❞

(The older sister of an ADHD sufferer)

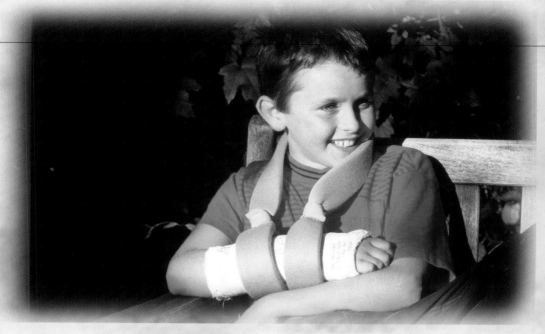

Who's ill? Who's normal?

Today, scientists and doctors are beginning to understand the causes of ADHD and other illnesses that affect how people behave. We have moved on from the days when all people who were mentally ill were locked up, but there is still a lot of prejudice about illnesses that affect the brain. It's hard not to view the difficult behaviour of a child with ADHD simply as naughtiness or laziness.

Children with ADHD do what many normal children do sometimes, but because they are ill they cannot stop themselves. For example, all young children rush about a lot. But a child with ADHD charges around like a racing car in overdrive. Children with

A broken arm attracts sympathy, but children with ADHD drive others mad.

ADHD are **hyperactive** compared with other children of the same age. All children find it difficult to pay attention to a teacher all the time, or to listen carefully to the instructions for playing a new computer game, but a child with ADHD finds it almost impossible. Children often act without thinking – they can sometimes be **impulsive**. But a child with ADHD may rush across a busy street even when his or her mother has explained a thousand times that it is dangerous. This behaviour is no more the child's fault than having an aching tooth or a broken arm, but it doesn't make those around them want to help. It makes them furious.

The history of ADHD

There are very few new diseases, but there are many new names for old ones. The more doctors and scientists understand about what causes healthy as well as unhealthy behaviour, the more detailed and accurate they become in describing and naming old conditions or illnesses.

In 400 BC, the Greek physician Hippocrates described people who had 'quickened responses to **sensory** experience, but were also less **tenacious** because the soul moves on quickly to the next impulse'. If you swap '**impulsive**' for 'quickened', put 'less able to concentrate' for 'less tenacious' and use '**hyperactive**' instead of the 'soul moving on quickly', you have the characteristics that make up a modern **diagnosis** of ADHD.

In 1902, a British children's doctor, George Still, noticed that a group of his patients – mostly boys – exhibited a pattern of difficult behaviour which had started before the age of eight.

The Greek physician Hippocrates, who lived 2500 years ago, described people who suffered from something very like ADHD.

These children were **inattentive**, hyperactive and resisted discipline. In the language of his time, Still said they showed 'lack of moral control' – we might say they were 'naughty'. Still's patients probably had ADHD plus another disorder called **oppositional defiant disorder** or **conduct disorder**, a condition that often accompanies ADHD (see page 12). Still believed that the cause of this behaviour was inborn, not down to bad parenting or bad environment. This is what doctors continue to believe today.

In 1918–19 there was a massive influenza (flu) epidemic. Flu can cause inflammation of the brain and many people who survived the illness developed ADHD-like symptoms. This led to the mistaken idea that ADHD is caused by brain damage.

In 1937, by a happy accident, Charles Bradley, a US doctor, used a **stimulant** drug called **amphetamine** to treat child patients who were in hospital because of their disturbed behaviour. Their behaviour improved – they calmed down and became more able to concentrate. This was unexpected, because stimulants normally make people livelier, more chatty and a bit careless. It took another twenty years for specially developed stimulants to become the first-line treatment for ADHD and for doctors to discover why they work in this way.

Over the next 50 years there was much debate about whether hyperactivity or inattention was more important, and about whether there were two different sorts of ADHD. Then, in 1987, the American Medical Association agreed on the name Attention Deficit Hyperactivity Disorder.

Some experts believe that the British war-time leader Winston Churchill may have had ADHD as a child.

Who is affected?

With few exceptions, estimates of how many people have a disease or disorder are informed guesswork. In the case of ADHD, all we can say with confidence is that the same percentage of children develops the illness wherever they live, whether they are rich or poor, and whatever culture they come from. However, in countries with less-developed health and education systems they are less likely to receive treatment for the condition. In the USA, the number of prescriptions written by doctors for the drugs that treat ADHD increased five fold in the 1990s. This is partly because doctors are getting better at recognizing the symptoms, so more children are now **diagnosed**, and also because sufferers continue on the drugs into adult life.

Most ADHD statistics come from the USA, but there have also been significant studies carried out in other places, including Australia, Brazil, Canada, Chile, China, Germany, India, Indonesia, Israel, Nigeria, Puerto Rico, Thailand and the UK.

How many are affected?

Estimates have been increasing. A safe estimate is probably four or five children in every one hundred aged between four and fourteen years old (conservative estimates suggest three in every one hundred). Estimates vary widely partly because the check-list of symptoms and signs used to diagnose the illness is not exactly the same in every country. Estimates also vary because what doctors consider 'normal' behaviour varies. For example, what Japanese and US doctors consider to be normal levels of **hyperactivity** in children, Chinese and Indonesian doctors rate as exceptional levels.

A child has the same chance of developing ADHD whatever country or culture he or she comes from.

Boys and girls

More boys are diagnosed with ADHD than girls – lots more. Again the exact figures vary, but at least three times as many boys as girls are diagnosed with the disorder, and possibly six times as many. Some experts think this is partly because it is more difficult to identify ADHD in girls because girls are generally less hyperactive.

How many grown-ups have ADHD?

The few studies that have followed child sufferers into adult life find that as many as three quarters still have symptoms as adults. Some symptoms, hyperactivity for example, become less severe with age, and those who have had treatment learn strategies and take medication. However, the condition cannot be cured altogether.

Symptoms and behaviours

People with ADHD can be dreamy or supercharged. This is because the four main behaviours that mark the condition – **inattention**, **distractibility**, **hyperactivity** and **impulsiveness** – don't always show up to an equal degree. Often either the first two are dominant, or the second two. Some people have both sets of symptoms, and all children with ADHD have problems with finishing homework, keeping their rooms tidy and getting on with other people.

As many as two-thirds of children with ADHD have other disorders that add to their problems. A third to a half may have **oppositional defiant disorder** (also known as **conduct disorder**). Basically this means they are not only inattentive and/or hyperactive, but they are also excessively uncooperative and get angry easily – what we might call 'stroppy' or 'cranky' (although people with these conditions cannot help it). Up to a quarter may also be anxious or depressed, and up to a third may have general problems with learning: with reading, writing and even with simple physical skills such as hitting balls or riding a bike.

It can be difficult to recognize a child with ADHD. Individual symptoms that make up their condition are seen in perfectly normal children. But someone with ADHD has a whole range of symptoms and the condition is a problem that cannot be overcome without help. Parents should try to remember this before coming out with some of the phrases discussed over the next few pages.

The Story of Fidgety Philip

The lines below come from a poem called 'The Story of Fidgety Philip'. The poem was written more than 150 years ago by a German doctor, Heinrich Hoffmann, who worked in what was then called a 'lunatic asylum'. Perhaps he had met some hyperactive children, because his description sums up well the behaviour of a child with ADHD.

> 'But fidgety Phil,
> He won't sit still;
> He wriggles,
> And giggles,
> And then I declare,
> Swung backwards and forwards,
> And tilts up his chair,
> Just like any rocking horse;
> "Philip! I am getting cross!"'

One condition, many names

ADHD in its lifetime has been called a lot of names: 'disorder', **'deficit'**, 'condition', **'syndrome'**. This reflects doctors' uncertainty about ADHD more than 100 years after it was first described. In the past ADHD has been called:

- Hyperactive Impulse Disorder
- Developmental Hyperactivity
- Minimal Brain **Dysfunction**
- Moral Control Deficit
- Hyperactive Child Syndrome
- Hyperkinetic Syndrome
- Minimal Brain Damage Syndrome
- Organic Drivenness

Many normal children show some of the symptoms of ADHD, but for sufferers the symptoms are more severe.

Inattentiveness and distractibility

'Everything I say goes in one ear and out the other.' Many ADHD sufferers cannot keep their attention focused for a moment, so you never know if they have heard what you said, or will do what you asked. However, ADHD sufferers are not consistently inattentive. Sometimes they are with you; sometimes they are on cloud nine. Some sufferers are distracted by their own thoughts; they are often bright, but sit quietly in class and learn little.

" He goes to his room to get ready for school and half an hour later he has one sock on and is looking out of the window. "

(Jane, the mother of an ADHD sufferer)

One hyperactive child can create chaos in a classroom.

Impulsiveness

'He's a nightmare on his bike; he has no road-sense.' When children act impulsively, they act before they think. No amount of reasoning does any good. They know what they are supposed to do, but ADHD sufferers are not in control of their instinctive impulses. Impulsive behaviour can be a particular worry because it makes children do things that are dangerous, such as climbing on roofs or waving sharp knives around. In class they interrupt and talk out of turn.

Hyperactivity

'I could never take him to a china department.' ADHD sufferers are often much more active than other children in their age group – some were hyperactive and demanding even when they were babies. In the playground, these children rampage like wild animals. Back in the classroom they find it impossible to sit still. At home they pace around, making everyone jumpy and exhausted.

Symptoms and behaviours

Social clumsiness

'She's hurt that her schoolmates shun her, but she brings it on herself.' Though many children with ADHD are sensitive and caring, others have no feeling for social rules. They'd love to be popular, but don't understand how to make friends. They often seem pushy or overbearing. Their impulses are so strong they don't notice the effect they are having on other people who think they are just bossy. They often say things or do things that are inappropriate or tactless.

Poor co-ordination

'He's so clumsy; he's the last one picked for any game.' Most children with ADHD have problems with 'fine motor skills' – things that require precision, like colouring, writing, and tying shoelaces. Some also have problems with 'gross motor skills' like riding a bike or catching a ball. Some are genuinely clumsy; others appear so because they do things thoughtlessly, on impulse. Some are both.

Disorganization

'He leaves a trail of lost property wherever he goes.' Most children are untidy or disorganized to some degree, but a child with ADHD could win trophies for creating chaos: clothes back to front; odd socks; messages from school that don't get delivered; lost books and, of course, a bedroom that looks as though an earthquake hit it.

"She's so disorganized she would eat a Mars Bar and clean her teeth at the same time."

(Gail, the mother of an ADHD sufferer)

Low self-esteem

'She's started to give up without even trying.' It is not surprising that, with all their problems, children with ADHD often suffer from low self-esteem. They are usually bright enough to see they are making a mess of things yet they just can't stop themselves. For a parent, one of the most heartbreaking things is to see how a child suffers from not being able to achieve. They want to win prizes and be chosen for the team. All children want to do well and for their parents to be proud of them. Children with ADHD sometimes seem doomed to failure.

Boundless but undirected energy is one of the many symptoms of ADHD.

Living with ADHD

First the bad news...

People with ADHD may feel confused, stupid, overloaded with information, lost and frustrated. Some sufferers feel that living with ADHD is like 'being put into a dark room with things scattered around to trip you. You don't get a flashlight ... but everyone else does. You trip around the room, bumping into things, until you finally learn the layout of the room. Then someone moves you to a new room, and the process starts again.'

Some people have compared the feeling to watching someone change the channels on the TV every few seconds. You can get a general idea of what is going on, but you miss most of the content. 'It's like having a whirlwind in your mind. Everything seems to be blowing around and nothing stays put.'

Brothers and sisters

ADHD is a condition that is tough on the child who has it, tough on parents and teachers, and equally tough on brothers and sisters too. Jenny has a younger brother with ADHD. She says 'It's not fair. He is always the centre of attention. We have to keep telling him how well he's doing, even when he's being a total idiot. Mum's put a lock on my door because before he was always coming in and breaking things and messing things up.'

People with ADHD may feel angry, misunderstood, left-out, picked on and different. Autumn is twelve years old and suffers from ADHD. She says that she never wanted to be **diagnosed** with ADHD and hates living with the condition. She says, 'I don't like to be treated different from anyone else but I am. My advice to other kids with ADHD is to set goals and have your dream, don't give up, you can do it too!'

And now the good news...

ADHD can be a positive influence too. People with ADHD can be curious, sensitive, creative, artistic, enthusiastic, athletic, imaginative, loving, funny and energetic. ADHD sufferers can have as much imagination as anyone else and some produce ideas and pictures which are highly original. The curiosity and boundless energy of ADHD **hyperactivity** can also be a plus when channelled into constructive activities.

For example, some successful businessmen and entrepreneurs exhibit the symptoms of ADHD, though they usually have a team of people behind them to compensate for their ADHD limitations.

ADHD sufferers express their creativity in many ways. They may paint, play the guitar, become music producers, actors or farmers. Communicating in words is often more difficult for them. One exception is Bob Seay of Colorado Springs, USA. He started writing at school and is now a successful

❝I was passing a field and was beckoned to photograph it by the inhabitants delicately swaying their petals to the vibration of the wind. They are rather magical ... sad ... beautiful ... mindful, perhaps.❞

'Poppies' by an ADHD sufferer and talented photographer. Someone with ADHD sees things differently, which makes the photographer's description of the scene both original and imaginative.

professional writer. Here, in a passage that is both original and chaotic, he vividly describes some of the many positive aspects of living with ADHD: 'See all of your worldly possessions at one time ... because they are all over the floor. (You are) ENTHUSIASTIC; Willing to take a Risk ... constantly surprised by finding clothing you had forgotten about. Able to tie seemingly unrelated ideas together ... In class popularity contests, always voted "Most Entertaining"; Blows up, but then usually recovers quickly; An unstoppable dynamo of human energy ... Provides job security for writers of Spell Check programs ...'

Nicky's story

Nicky lives in Lincolnshire, UK. As a young child, he was hyperactive and impulsive, but it wasn't until he went to school that he was diagnosed as having ADHD. He was prescribed **stimulant** drugs, which helped keep his symptoms under control, but Nicky still had difficulty with his school work. 'Things got calmer,' says his father, Gerry, 'but he was never going to be a university professor.' But then Nicky discovered gardening. Plants, soil types, bugs, climate and cultivation became his doorway to study. At eighteen he got a place at agricultural college and hopes to become a market gardener.

The untamed energy of a hyperactive child may be channelled into physical and creative achievement.

Living with ADHD

Jamie's story

Jamie is the youngest of three boys in a family from Sussex, UK and he always lived in the shadow of his older, brighter brothers. When questions were asked, they were quick to answer, so Jamie never bothered. He wasn't interested in school work, had a problem with reading and writing and was diagnosed with mild **dyslexia**. Then when he was about twelve, he was diagnosed with ADHD. Sarah, Jamie's mother, says:

'He was always in trouble both at school and home. He didn't walk from room to room, he jumped, ran, lunged or rolled on the floor. He would pick things up and hurl them around. Outside, if there was gravel, he'd scoop up handfuls and throw it, with no thought for the consequences. Many windows were broken.

'At school, he lost things, forgot what he was doing and couldn't concentrate for five minutes. He seemed oblivious – in a world of his own. If he was sucked into a favourite TV programme, he'd be totally focused, but once it finished, all hell broke loose again.

'Eventually the school's educational psychologist assessed Jamie for ADHD and, with some difficulty, we persuaded him to take Ritalin. I was sceptical of faddish 'designer' drugs and couldn't believe it would work. But it was miraculous. He underwent a total behaviour change. He became focused, able to concentrate, walked normally and he was no longer anti-social. Of course he often forgot to take his pills – a common symptom of ADHD – and I always knew immediately, as his old behaviour would resurface.

'For Jamie and all of us, it was a life-saver. He's now 21, has a job he enjoys in construction and is quite the perfectionist – a craftsman in the making.'

Jamie says:
'I hated school. I was in the special needs group. I had to be taken out of class for special tuition. It made me feel different. When I took my Ritalin tablets, it was embarrassing as I had to go to the school secretary to get them – when I remembered that is! Ritalin helped me concentrate on what the teacher was saying. I felt calmer too. For me school was a waste of time. Everything I've learnt came from my family, mates and just living. I just like … to be outside – sea fishing is terrific and they don't teach that at school!'

Like Jamie, many ADHD sufferers are able to focus briefly on their favourite TV programme, but not for long.

What causes ADHD?

In the past there was little understanding of the way plants or animals worked. Doctors described mental disorders but were in the dark about what caused them or even what part of the body had gone wrong. These days we are able to study the living brain. First came imaging techniques that showed the structures of the brain. However, this did not help explain what caused ADHD because the brains of those with ADHD have the same structures as normal brains (although recent research suggests that certain parts can be smaller).

Then, in the late 1980s, new ways of imaging the brain were invented that showed what was *happening* in the brain and doctors discovered that there were differences in the brains of people with ADHD. In addition, doctors learned more about how illnesses are passed on, by infection for example, from one person to another, or from parent to child in the genes. This gave scientists and doctors real insight into the causes and nature of conditions like ADHD that affect the way people feel, think and behave.

Understanding of how certain conditions are handed down from parent to child in genes has increased enormously in recent years.

In the genes

If you look at the families of children with ADHD you usually discover at least one close relative with a similar problem: a father who was always in trouble at school; a cousin who was hopeless at lessons; an uncle who was always getting into fights. The identical twin of an ADHD sufferer, who comes from the same egg and is made of the same **genetic** material, will almost always (in 90 per cent of cases) share the condition.

This evidence tells us that ADHD is hereditary – that is to say it is passed down from parent to child in their genes. Genes are little pieces of information contained in the material of every cell of the body that convey instructions for building each unique individual, making him or her grow and function. Genes do not explain everything about why some people develop an illness and others do not, but they explain a lot.

Environmental factors

Genes make people more or less likely to get certain diseases or to suffer more severely. Upbringing and surroundings also play a part. For example, a child with ADHD whose parents are very sympathetic, whose school is supportive, and whose family and friends are accepting will do better than one whose parents are irritable or hostile, whose teachers are critical and who is rejected by all around.

A supportive environment makes a child more likely to overcome the disadvantages of having ADHD.

What causes ADHD?

The normal brain

The human brain is constantly bombarded with information: all the things you see, hear and feel. The brain also gets messages from inside the body (such as whether you are hungry, or whether you are getting a cold) and from your memory (for example, who people are). It's rather like hearing several radio stations overlapping one another.

The brain copes with the potential overload by selecting messages that are important and dumping the rest. To do this, several specialist regions of the brain work together. The command centre of the brain tells different parts of the brain what information to accelerate and deliver and what to filter out. The other parts of the brain carry out these instructions. The brain's command centre is known as the **frontal lobes** (at the front of the head, behind the forehead).

ADHD brains

In the brain of someone with ADHD, information floods in without much filtering. It's a bit like watching a split-screen television with lots of different scenes pictured all at the same time. Information is recorded, but because there is so much of it, the child may respond **impulsively** without weighing up the consequences. Alternatively, he or she may not respond to any of the messages crowding his or her brain. He or she is either impulsive or **inattentive** – or possibly both.

The brain of an ADHD sufferer endures unfiltered information overload. Sometimes it seems impossible to cope.

Images of the brain

The latest imaging techniques scan the brain to show where there is activity and where there is not. One technique, called **SPECT (Single Photon Emission Computed Tomography)**, measures the blood flow to different parts of the brain. Another technique, **PET (Positron Emission Tomography)** picks out tiny sugar **molecules**, tagged with a radioactive marker so that they will show up under the scan. The sugar collects in the areas of the brain that are most active and makes them 'light up'. By showing whether the lights are either on or off in significant areas, SPECT and PET scans tell us three things about the brains of people with ADHD:

- the frontal lobes (command centre) of the brain are under-active in the ADHD brain compared to a normal brain
- those areas that collect visual and sound information are massively overloaded, suggesting that much unnecessary information is not being filtered out
- when **stimulant** drugs are taken these differences usually disappear.

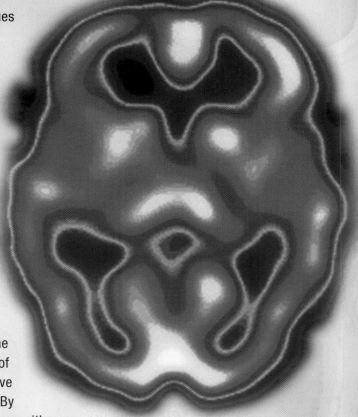

SPECT images reveal the location of brain activity by picking out the blood flow to different areas. This is an image of a normal brain. Some differences seen in SPECT images of the brains of ADHD sufferers can be corrected with drugs.

Neurotransmitters: the brain's messengers

It is an oversimplification to think of the brain as having just one command centre and regions that carry out orders. The brain also acts as a whole – a bit like an electronic synthesizer producing a complex musical sound composed of many superimposed tracks.

In the brain, billions of different specialist cells pass messages to one another, a bit like a telephone exchange or a computer. These cells – **neurons** – communicate with each other by means of chemical messengers called **neurotransmitters**.

Between each brain cell is a small gap called a **synapse**. When a neuron wants to send a message to a neighbour it releases a neurotransmitter which crosses the synapse and stimulates its neighbouring cell. The process sparks a chain reaction between brain cells. More than 50 different types of neurotransmitter have been identified, each one controlling different behaviours or feelings, and active in different regions of the brain.

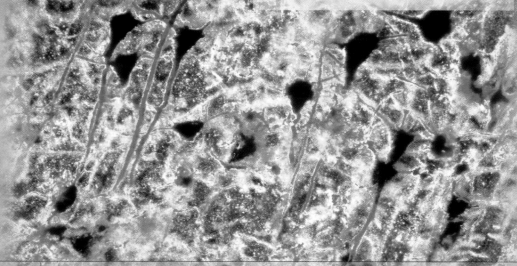

This image of a section through part of the brain is magnified so that you can see individual cells (neurons), which show up black in the picture. Neurons communicate by releasing various neurotransmitters that stimulate neighbouring cells.

Dopamine and noradrenaline

The problems associated with ADHD are caused by an imbalance of the chemical messengers **dopamine** and **noradrenaline** in the frontal lobes (the command centre) and other important regions of the brain. Noradrenaline is known as **norepinephrine** in some countries.

Without sufficient dopamine, the child with ADHD cannot pick out the important messages from the flood of information bombarding the brain. The child cannot filter out the irrelevant 'background noise' and focus on what matters. Children with ADHD do not have sufficient dopamine, but too much dopamine is also a bad thing. People with too much become obsessive: they concentrate too much on one thing – trying to keep their hands clean, for example, even when they're not dirty.

Noradrenaline has a different role. It is the chemical messenger that prompts 'fight or flight' reactions – the instinct of animals in a tight corner either to fight or run away. Noradrenaline gears you up, makes you ready for action. Too little makes people indifferent and

Too little of the neurotransmitter dopamine in one important area of the brain makes it difficult for ADHD sufferers to focus their attention.

bored; too much makes them crave excitement – even when this is inappropriate or even dangerous. When these two important brain chemicals are out of balance someone will have difficulty in paying attention and/or be impulsive and hyperactive.

Dopamine levels

Dopamine levels go up when you are happy and relaxed. The evidence comes from people stroking their pets. Scientists in South Africa found that both dogs and their owners had lower blood pressure and higher dopamine levels after they had been relaxing together for half an hour.

What causes ADHD?

Upbringing and environment

The principal cause of ADHD is an abnormality in brain function that affects behaviour. This abnormality is inherited – in other words, it is genetic. However, other factors also need to be considered.

During the last century, experts began to stress the importance of upbringing and environment as factors that help children grow up healthy and happy. Environment, we now know, is every bit as important as the genes inherited from parents. Even conditions like ADHD, which has a known genetic cause, are affected by environment. The behaviour of parents, family and teachers especially can make things better or worse.

However, it can sometimes be difficult for parents of ADHD sufferers to remain constantly patient. Difficult children – even those who are not ill – can make their parents feel inadequate. And, since ADHD runs in families, one parent may also be struggling with ADHD problems.

Problems at birth

It is often the case that the mother of a child with ADHD had a difficult pregnancy or childbirth. It is also believed that there is a higher risk of a child being born with ADHD if the mother smokes or is exposed to some industrial poisons, like those in weed killers, during pregnancy. If the baby is seriously undernourished after birth the likelihood will also increase.

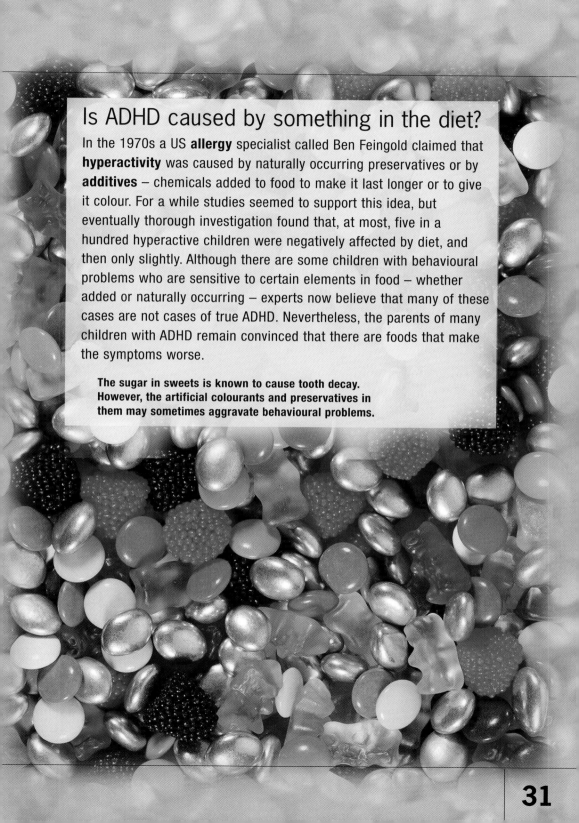

Is ADHD caused by something in the diet?

In the 1970s a US **allergy** specialist called Ben Feingold claimed that **hyperactivity** was caused by naturally occurring preservatives or by **additives** – chemicals added to food to make it last longer or to give it colour. For a while studies seemed to support this idea, but eventually thorough investigation found that, at most, five in a hundred hyperactive children were negatively affected by diet, and then only slightly. Although there are some children with behavioural problems who are sensitive to certain elements in food – whether added or naturally occurring – experts now believe that many of these cases are not cases of true ADHD. Nevertheless, the parents of many children with ADHD remain convinced that there are foods that make the symptoms worse.

The sugar in sweets is known to cause tooth decay. However, the artificial colourants and preservatives in them may sometimes aggravate behavioural problems.

Diagnosing ADHD

Before doctors treat anyone they must be sure what they're treating. This process is called **diagnosis**. Basically this means 'putting a name to it'. It's also called 'evaluation'. It's especially important in ADHD because the behaviours that define the illness – **inattention**, **distractibility**, **hyperactivity** and **impulsiveness** – are present to some degree in all children. Doctors must be sure that these behaviours are abnormal for the child's age group. In addition, the mix of symptoms varies from patient to patient and 50 per cent of those with ADHD also suffer from other behaviour problems on top of their ADHD. These include **conduct disorder** or **oppositional defiant disorder** (being obstructive or defiant), learning difficulties (difficulty reading and writing) or motor disorders (extreme clumsiness and difficulty with physical co-ordination).

❝The eye of the experienced beholder is more important than a laboratory-load of tests.❞

(Dr Christopher Green and Dr Kit Chee, *Understanding ADHD*, 1997)

Specialists make a diagnosis by checking a child's symptoms against standard questionnaires and by testing their behaviour.

The diagnosis of ADHD is carried out by medical experts, but the first alarm bells are usually sounded by a concerned parent or teacher – often because of underperformance at school. Specialists use a number of techniques to arrive at a diagnosis, but these are usually:

- noting symptoms that show up in the home and school environment
- studying a detailed medical and behavioural history of the child and the family
- testing the child against some **objective** yardstick: the most

widely used are tick-lists or questionnaires. There are also computer programs that measure how a child performs simple tests and others that analyse brainwaves (electrical activity in various key areas of the brain).

Only after all other problems have been ruled out, and the exact kind of ADHD from which the child suffers has been determined – i.e., inattentiveness/distractibility with or without hyperactivity and impulsiveness – will the specialist begin to plan a treatment programme.

Conditions sometimes confused or combined with ADHD

Experts also attempt to distinguish between children with behavioural difficulties who *don't* have ADHD, and ADHD sufferers who have other conditions as well. These conditions are: **autism**, or it's milder form, **Asperger's syndrome**; epilepsy; specific learning disabilities; hearing disability; depression; brain injury; family **dysfunction** (when the behaviour of the whole family is the problem); and of course the normally active child whose parents are at their wits' end.

Treatment programmes

There is at the moment no cure for ADHD. When a child is **diagnosed** his or her family knows that they will all have to live with ADHD for the rest of their lives. But there are ways to overcome the symptoms of the condition. The best results come from combining more than one treatment in a programme that includes the child, the family and teachers.

Specialists who can help

There are various educational and medical specialists who can offer help and advise sufferers of ADHD and their families. These include special needs teachers, counsellors, educational psychologists, behavioural psychologists, **occupational therapists**, paediatricians (doctors specializing in looking after children), **psychotherapists** and child psychiatrists. In an ideal world children with ADHD would have a team of specialists at their disposal, and sophisticated machines to monitor their progress. In practice, it is generally parents and teachers who cope, guided by specialists, books and support organizations.

Drugs plus behaviour modification

In most cases, the medication doctors prescribe rapidly makes ADHD more manageable. The most successful drugs come from a family called **stimulants**. Stimulants enable children with ADHD to focus on what is important, retain what they're told, and hold back that impulse to charge ahead without considering the consequences.

Behaviour modification ('mod' for short), is a term used to describe professional psychologists' formal version of what many parents and teachers do when bringing up children. This involves teaching them useful and rewarding ways to control or change their behaviour. For example, they might say 'Put your homework in your bag tonight. That way you won't leave it behind tomorrow.' Children can usually be taught simple ways to change their behaviour by a mixture of rules, rewards and punishment. But because children with ADHD don't think ahead, or anticipate either positive or negative outcomes, they require specially designed programmes. These use repetition, regularity and endless patience to put them in control.

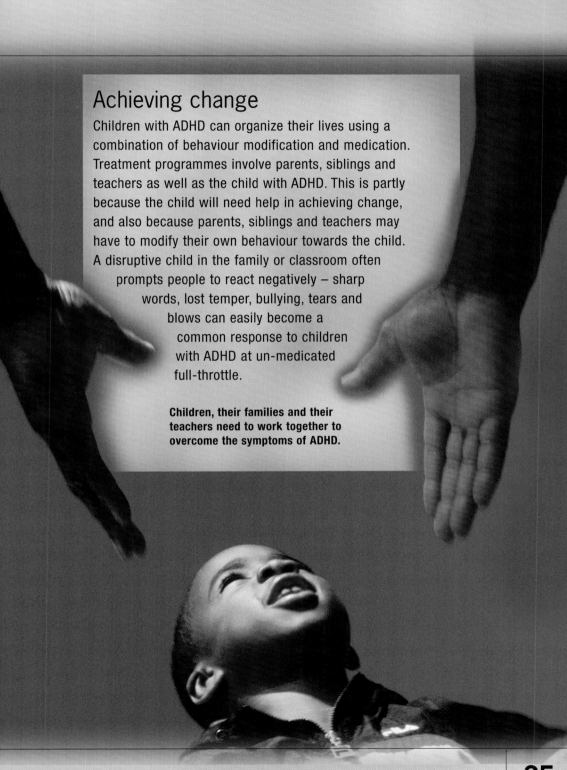

Achieving change

Children with ADHD can organize their lives using a combination of behaviour modification and medication. Treatment programmes involve parents, siblings and teachers as well as the child with ADHD. This is partly because the child will need help in achieving change, and also because parents, siblings and teachers may have to modify their own behaviour towards the child. A disruptive child in the family or classroom often prompts people to react negatively – sharp words, lost temper, bullying, tears and blows can easily become a common response to children with ADHD at un-medicated full-throttle.

Children, their families and their teachers need to work together to overcome the symptoms of ADHD.

Behaviour modification at home

A basic rule of **behaviour modification** is: 'Behaviour that is not rewarded disappears. Rewarded, it will persist.' The difficulty with children with ADHD is that they can't wait for a reward in the future, they need it immediately. So rewards must be small and be given often. A 'gold star' system of rewards allows a child to earn rewards frequently, but the rewards can also add up to a bigger reward. For example, if a child collects enough stars, then they might get to go bowling.

A regular routine

All children benefit from routine. If they do the same things at the same time every day, eventually they will do them automatically. Routine is absolutely vital for children with ADHD who have problems paying attention to instructions and remembering them.

Laying down and enforcing rules

Parents and teachers need to lay down rules, because rules sidestep argument. If a child asks 'Can I watch television?', the response might be 'Not until your homework's finished – that's the rule.'

A system of carefully graduated rewards may help combat an ADHD sufferer's tendency to disorganization.

But rules need to be enforced, so parents must agree a penalty and enforce it if that rule is broken, keeping firm, calm and matter-of-fact.

Making lists

Everyone uses lists to jog the memory. Lists help a child with ADHD to keep his or her room tidy, complete homework and finish all the tasks that, unaided, he or she will probably forget. Lists can also help with particular problems: for example, 'Things to do if I feel fidgety' or 'Things to do if I'm about to lose my cool'.

Knowing the danger signals

Parents of children with ADHD get to know the events that risk aggravating their child's symptoms. These might be parties, late nights, visitors, long car journeys, or any change in the daily routine. These events cannot be avoided, but measures can be planned. If the child is on medication, for example, doctors may recommend a slightly higher dose to help overcome these situations.

Long car journeys

The backseat of a car is often a battleground on long journeys. Special measures are required if one of the passengers has ADHD:

- lay down rules: no teasing or tormenting and agree penalties if rules are broken
- plan regular breaks and give regular countdowns to the next one
- make sure each child has his or her own toy
- devise games – winning points or sweets for spotting things along the road such as animals, particular models of car or road signs
- put a large piece of luggage between the occupants of the back seat to reduce opportunities for poking or provoking.

Behaviour modification at school

Some fortunate pupils with ADHD and their teachers get help and advice from an educational psychologist or special needs teacher. Ideally, a child with ADHD would have the undivided attention of his own teacher or be taught in a small group – but this is unlikely in most ordinary schools. But even in a class of 30, a teacher who understands the problems associated with ADHD can do much to help.

Wherever possible, teachers try to give children with ADHD one-to-one attention.

Capturing the child's attention

A teacher can use a wide variety of measures to capture the attention of a child with ADHD. These may include sitting the child at the front of class, between two quiet pupils, maintaining eye-contact, using animated gestures, and varying the pace and volume of his or her voice to project enthusiasm and excitement. Keeping things short and snappy and asking the child lots of questions also helps to keep him or her involved in the lesson.

Help with organization and memory

A teacher can help a child with ADHD to be more organized by writing things down, on paper or the blackboard, and by encouraging the child to make lists. It also helps if the teacher breaks up what the child must do into manageable parts and suggests a set amount of time for each task. In lessons, the teacher may start with an outline and then go into detail. A teacher may also use mnemonics (tricks to jog the memory) and list key words or figures.

Providing support

By understanding that strict discipline does not work for children with ADHD, teachers can help by being firm but tolerant of the child's lapses. Teachers may also show support by giving specific praise: 'That's an interesting subject to write about' rather than 'That's a good essay.' Teachers can also show their support by keeping an eye out for bullying or teasing incidents, and, above all, by never losing their cool.

Working together

By keeping in touch personally (written notes often get lost!), teachers and parents can ensure that the rules the child lives by are consistent, whether these are to do with homework, taking his or her medication, or what he or she must wear and bring to school. By sharing the child's problems and progress, parents and teachers can decide if specialist help – counselling, medical advice or special needs teaching – is needed.

Treating ADHD with drugs

ADHD is a condition that affects the brain. Drugs that affect the brain are called psychotropic, which means 'mind-changing'. Alcohol and the nicotine in cigarettes are psychotropic drugs – they change mood and behaviour. The drugs with the longest track record of being successful in treating the symptoms of ADHD come from a family of psychotropic drugs called **stimulants**. Stimulants usually make people wakeful and excited. However, as we have seen, they also have the effect of enabling ADHD sufferers to concentrate better and control **impulsive** behaviour. They work well for between 70 and 90 per cent of those with the condition.

Occasionally other drugs may be prescribed instead of, or in addition to, stimulants. Anti-depressants (which relieve depression) and some non-stimulant drugs can, in some cases, have a beneficial effect on one or more of the symptoms of ADHD.

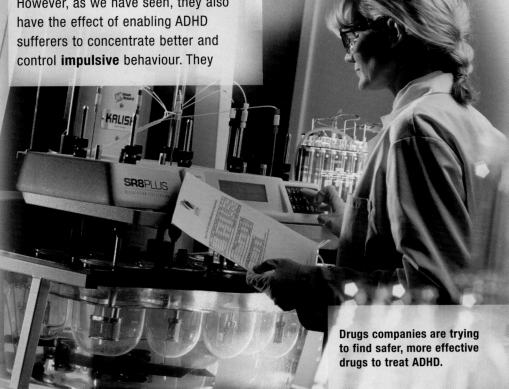

Drugs companies are trying to find safer, more effective drugs to treat ADHD.

How do stimulants work?

For years doctors did not understand why stimulants had an effect on people with ADHD that is opposite to the effect they have on everyone else. They now know that stimulants affect the levels of the **neurotransmitters** (the chemical messengers through which **neurons** communicate) **dopamine** and **noradrenaline** (also known as **norepinephrine**) in those areas of the brain that sift and select important information for attention and control the urge to take action.

Stimulants work fast, taking effect in 15 to 30 minutes. However, the dose that will be effective has to be worked out for each person individually, because the time it takes the drug to affect the neurotransmitters varies. Stimulants cease to work after four or five hours, so most children need to take them two or three times a day. Medication is now also available that is released slowly over several hours. This means that children with ADHD do not have to take tablets in front of their friends at school.

The naming of drugs

Even doctors find it difficult to recognize the names of drugs. The names belong to no real, spoken language but are invented by the people who develop them. In addition, they have at least two names: the name of their active chemical, and a trade name that varies from country to country. The most common medication for ADHD has the chemical name **methylphenidate**, but the names you will hear most often are its trade names: Ritalin, Equasym (UK) and Metadate (USA). The first 12-hour extended release drug has the trade name Concerta. You may also hear the chemical name of an older group of stimulants, the **amphetamines** or **dexamphetamines** (trade name Dexadrine).

Treating ADHD with drugs

The stimulant family

We all know families that include a bad uncle, or perhaps a tearaway big brother. Few families are without them. It's like that with the stimulant family: some stimulants, such as caffeine, are mild; some, such as Ritalin, are medically useful; others, such as cocaine, are dangerous, and often have a frightful reputation.

Just because the stimulant used to treat ADHD has some disreputable relations, it does not mean it is equally bad. Although there is a family resemblance, different stimulants vary in their precise chemical composition, and this makes them behave differently in the body. Cocaine is addictive:

people who use it develop a need for it, can't do without it, and have to take more and more to get the same effect. Caffeine is extremely mild: it would take gallons of coffee to achieve the effect of more powerful stimulants like methylphenidate and dexamphetamine which are used to treat ADHD. And stimulants that are used to treat ADHD are not addictive when used at the dose prescribed, nor do they make children more likely to grow up to become addicted to other drugs – quite the reverse. When people with ADHD do not receive treatment, they may then be more likely to try harmful drugs because their lives are often in a mess.

Drug treatments give children with ADHD a chance to reveal what they can really do – a bit like glasses for the short-sighted.

ff When I take medication I can control my ADHD, my ADHD doesn't control me. It helps me fit in with my school friends and be accepted like everybody else. JJ

(James, an ADHD sufferer)

Side effects

All drugs have *some* side effects which affect *some* patients. About 10 per cent of ADHD patients suffer side effects with the most widely prescribed drugs. Side effects mostly occur at the beginning of treatment before the right dose has been established. They include loss of appetite, difficulty in sleeping, and occasionally tearfulness or irritability.

Loss of self-esteem

In most cases, when children take prescribed stimulants the problems they have faced become more manageable. The problem is that parents and teachers may give the impression that this is all the drug's doing, making the child feel incompetent. In fact, the drug is allowing the child's true level of ability to emerge and parents should reassure children that this is real, not a product of the drug. People should remember that taking pills is a bit like wearing glasses or having a brace on your teeth, so there is no need to feel singled out or 'sick'.

Can modifying the diet help?

The ancient physician Hippocrates thought that if you had the symptoms of ADHD you should eat 'barley rather than wheat ... and fish rather than meat'. The idea that illness can be caused and cured by diet is still popular today, after 2500 years. The discovery of food **allergies** and **intolerances** has encouraged people still further to look for cures that involve changing the food that sufferers eat.

ADHD is no exception. Throughout the 1970s the Feingold Diet, devised by the US allergy specialist Ben Feingold, was thought to be the answer to **hyperactivity**. Feingold recommended avoiding not only artificial **additives** but also natually occuring preservatives in food.

However there is little evidence that anything in food has an effect on levels of

inattention or impulsive behaviour in children with ADHD, although in a few cases it may have some on levels of hyperactivity. Of course, children with ADHD may also have an allergy. If a parent feels that a particular food is aggravating their child's ADHD

Salicylates, which occur naturally in strawberries and oranges, can cause an allergic reaction and occasionally aggravate the symptoms of ADHD.

symptoms the child may be put on what is called an **exclusion diet**. He or she starts by eating a very bland, known-to-be harmless diet: for example, water, pear juice, unseasoned meat and preservative-free bread.

If their behaviour improves, other foods are added one at a time until the ones causing the problem are clearly identified. Then a diet is adopted that avoids all the troublesome foods.

Troublesome foods

The following foods may sometimes aggravate ADHD:

- salicylates: these are found in a range of natural foods – strawberries, oranges, tomatoes and pineapple – as well as in flavourings, cola drinks and in the widely used drug, aspirin
- amines: these are chemicals created when food is broken down by fermentation – found in wine, beer, yeast, cheese, chocolate, fish products, cola drinks and ripe, mushy fruit (for example, bananas and avocados)
- monosodium glutamate (MSG): this chemical is found in wheat and many other grains; it is used to improve flavour, notably in Chinese food
- food additives: these include preservatives, added to make food last longer; and colourings, added to make it look attractive.

Alternative treatments

Parents are naturally worried about giving their children drugs – especially **stimulants**, which sometimes have a bad reputation. Many parents prefer the idea of a treatment that is 'natural', although this may be little more than a word used on the packaging of a product. Some remedies promoted for ADHD certainly do no harm, as long as they are not regarded as a substitute for proven, successful medication.

These days, the Internet provides information about all sorts of alternative cures to prescription medicines. Most of these 'natural' products are still manufactured, but they do not undergo the rigorous research – dose testing and investigation into side effects and their interaction with other drugs – that

prescription drugs must go through before they are allowed on the market.

Talking therapies

A 'talking therapy' is a treatment that involves a patient discussing with a trained therapist what they feel and how to change how they feel or behave. This is often helpful. However, many people with ADHD may not have sufficient control over their behaviour to benefit from it unless they first take their stimulants so that they can focus on the discussion. Some talking therapies tried for ADHD are: **psychotherapy**, **cognitive behaviour therapy**, social skills training (training in socially acceptable behaviour or good manners), and counselling (non-specialist discussion aimed at helping the patient).

Many unusual treatments have been suggested for treating ADHD. One is to swing in a hammock, which certainly does no harm!

Occupational therapy

Occupational therapists help children with ADHD who have problems with practical physical skills like writing, playing ball, and tying shoelaces. Like other therapies this works better when combined with medication.

Parenting skills training

Parenting skills training aims to help family members cope with the problems of living with a child who has ADHD. Together they have training sessions to learn how to respond constructively.

Bio-feedback

In bio-feedback, patients are wired up to a machine that records brainwaves and shown how to control them by conjuring up certain thoughts and feelings. Children with ADHD may be too **impulsive** or **inattentive** to master the technique, so may not benefit from this treatment.

Eye exercises

Slow readers often have their sight tested. There is no evidence that ADHD children are more likely to have eye problems than other children, but eye exercises may be tried.

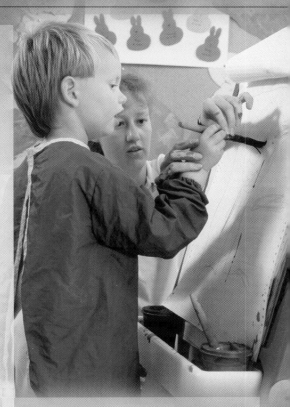

An occupational therapist helps children cope with the physical problems of ADHD.

More unusual treatments

Some of the unusual things tried for treating ADHD have included: cranial (skull) manipulation and realignment of the neck, skull realignment, tinted lenses and swinging in a hammock. Most of these have not been tested by thorough research.

Adults with ADHD

Many conditions get less severe with age – for example, asthma. This appears to be true of some symptoms of ADHD (including **hyperactivity**). For many years it was thought that ADHD corrected itself as children got older. Then the doctors treating children noticed that there was often an adult in the family who had recognizably similar problems.

ADHD emerges when children go to school partly because, between the ages of four and eighteen, we expect them to sit at desks and study most of the day. In the past, children were expected to learn the practical, physical skills of their parents – hunting, fishing, farming and caring for animals. It seems possible that the symptoms of ADHD might not have been such a severe handicap for those children as they are for children learning to read, write and do sums. And in hunting, the energy and disregard of danger of someone who is hyperactive might even be an advantage.

These days, adults with ADHD may still find jobs that don't require them to sit still or concentrate upon one thing for a long time. Some famous actors show the symptoms of ADHD, as do some sportspeople. Some people who are hopeless at school, like the former British prime minister Winston Churchill, nevertheless have successful careers in later life.

Those who are **diagnosed** in childhood can choose to continue with their medication and hopefully will also have learned ways to cope with ADHD behaviours. However, in the USA, 40 per cent of boys with *untreated* ADHD commit a crime by the time they reach sixteen and more than half (of those untreated) have drug or alcohol problems.

No one ever says it will be easy. Adults with ADHD are often haunted by a sense of failure or inadequacy. They may work twice as hard to achieve the same result as a person who does not have ADHD, and become workaholics. They are often not as easy to be with and have problems keeping jobs and partners.

Albert's story

Albert was slow to talk and a very poor learner at school. His work was messy, he was easily distracted and he never paid attention or joined in during class. He seemed to live in a dream. As an adult he never had great success in his personal relationships, but while working in the Swiss patent office he started to publish original scientific papers. He won worldwide fame with his revolutionary theories of relativity, and was awarded the 1921 Nobel Prize for Physics. His name was Albert Einstein!

Many experts believe that Albert Einstein had to overcome the obstacles of having ADHD. He was not a success at school, but nevertheless went on to win a Nobel Prize.

ADHD research and the future

In science, understanding the precise mechanism of an illness is often followed by improved treatment. Throughout the world there is more research into ADHD than almost any other mental disorder. The chief focus of attention is on the genes that increase the risk of developing ADHD.

Identifying genes

By comparing the genes of people who have ADHD with those of people who are unaffected, scientists have discovered slight variations in some genes that increase the risk of getting ADHD. Two genes affect the behaviour of **neurons** (nerve cells) so that they take up too much of the chemical messenger **dopamine**, causing a shortage in key areas of the brain. This excessive take-up of dopamine is blocked by **stimulants** such as **methylphenidate**. Genes that affect the balance of other **neurotransmitters** in the brain are also being investigated. Better understanding will eventually lead to new, improved treatments.

New drugs

A recent breakthrough has been the development of a non-stimulant drug for ADHD that works a bit like methylphenidate by correcting the balance of neurotransmitters in the brain. This new drug has recently been released in the USA and will soon be available in the UK. It is called atomoxetine (trade name: Strattera) and appears to work as well as methylphenidate with reduced side effects such as loss of appetite and sleeplessness. Nevertheless, it will be many years before the new drug builds up a track record comparable to the old tried and tested ones.

Designing a supportive environment for ADHD

Meanwhile, improvements are being made in other forms of treatment for ADHD. For example, we know that, although upbringing and the environment are not the cause of ADHD, they can make things better or worse. Research shows that a negative environment – one where families or schools are hostile and critical – increases the chance that a child with

ADHD will grow up to be a troubled adolescent and adult. When families are trained not to react with anger and hostility to children with ADHD, their symptoms are often reduced.

The future for ADHD sufferers is still uncertain. However, greater understanding provides hope that things will improve. This understanding is already contributing to better and earlier **diagnosis**, and to improved drugs and treatment options. Ultimately, it may contribute to the development of a cure.

When families are trained to support their children with ADHD, these children have a better chance of growing up to become well-adjusted adults.

Information and advice

A great deal of information about ADHD is available on the web. General background information can be obtained and also detailed information about symptoms and treatments.

Contacts in the UK

adders.org
Email: support@adders.org
Website: www.adders.org
This UK organization promotes awareness of ADHD and provides information, practical help and support to sufferers and their families in the UK and around the world.

ADDISS
10 Station Road, Mill Hill
London NW7 2JU
Tel: 020 8906 9068
E-mail: info@addiss.co.uk
Website: www.addiss.co.uk
The UK National Attention Deficit Disorder Information and Support Service provides information and resources about ADHD to parents, sufferers, teachers and health professionals. They hold training days for teachers and organize a large annual three-day conference for parents and professionals. They also have a large number of affiliated parent support groups.

ADHD UK Alliance
209–211 City Road
London EC1V 1JN
Tel: 020 7608 8760
Email: info@adhdalliance.org.uk
Website: www.adhdalliance.co.uk
This UK ADHD organization aims to raise public awareness of ADHD and improve services for sufferers and their families.

Contacts in the USA

ADDA
(Attention Deficit Disorder Association)
PO Box 543
Pottstown, PA 19464
Tel: 484-945-2101
Email: mail@add.org
Website: www.add.org
This is a comprehensive site, chiefly for adults but with a special 'Kids' corner' and pages for creative writing and pictures.

CHADD
(Children and Adults with Attention Deficit/Hyperactivity Disorder)
8181 Professional Place
Suite 150, Landover, MD 20785
Tel: 800-233-4050
Email: national@chadd.org
Website: www.chadd.org
This is the main US support organization for children and adults with ADHD. It offers a comprehensive range of material.

Contacts in Canada

ADDSA
(Attention Deficit Disorder Support Association)
242 Osborne Avenue
New Westminster, BC, V3L1Y8
Email: addsa@vcn.bc.ca
This support organization does not have a website of its own, but various regional 'chapters' can be found on different Canadian university sites.

Contacts in Australia

ADDISS
PO Box 1661 Milton, Brisbane, Queensland 4064
Tel: 617-3368-3977
Email: addiss@bigpond.com.au
Website: www.users.bigpond.com/addiss/
This organization provides information and support services to ADHD sufferers and their families in Australia.

Contacts in New Zealand

ADHD.org.nz
c/o ADDvocate NZ Inc., PO Box 249, Tauranga
Email: addvocate@xtra.co.nz
www.adhd.org.nz
This on-line support group site provides simple explanations, professional advice and rights.

Other useful websites

addconsults
www.addconsults.com
This site offers access to professional advice, articles about ADHD, news of conferences, and features chat, amazing stories, poems and paintings by children and adults with ADHD.

adhd.com
www.adhd.com
This site is geared to sufferers and families. It gives professional advice, has a chat room and features poems and pictures by ADHD children.

adhd.kids.com
http://adhd.kids.tripod.com
This is an original website for 'misunderstood children who thrive outside the box' – the box being the conventional classroom. It offers a space for talented children with ADHD or related problems to express themselves.

Further reading

Understanding ADHD: A Parent's Guide to Attention Deficit Hyperactivity Disorder in Children, by Dr Christopher Green and Dr Kit Chee; Vermillion, 1997

Putting on the Brakes: Young People's Guide to Understanding Attention Deficit Hyperactivity Disorder, by Patricia O. Quinn and Judith M. Stern; Magination Press, 2002

Learning To Slow Down and Pay Attention: A Book for Kids About ADD, by Kathleen G. Nadeau and Ellen B. Dixon; Magination Press, 1997

The Other Me: Poetic Thoughts on ADD for Adults, Kids and Parents, by Wilma R. Fellman; Specialty Press, 1997

Glossary

additive
something added, usually to commercial foods to preserve them or add colour

allergy
abnormal reaction to a food or something in the environment

amphetamine
type of stimulant drug

Asperger's syndrome
mild form of autism

autism
brain condition that causes children to be withdrawn and unable to relate normally to other people

behaviour modification
treating a problem by teaching new ways of behaving

cognitive behaviour therapy
treating a problem by teaching new ways of thinking

conduct disorder (also known as oppositional defiant disorder)
uncooperative, obstructive and disobedient behaviour

deficit
shortage of something; disability or illness

dexamphetamine
type of stimulant drug

diagnosis
identification of a disease by known symptoms or objective tests

distractible
easily distracted; having difficulty in focusing on one thing

dopamine
chemical messenger in the brain that aids selective attention

dysfunction
abnormality in the way something functions

dyslexia
disorder involving difficulty in learning to read or interpret words, letters and other symbols

exclusion diet
diet that involves the removal of all risk-prone foods, and the gradual inclusion of foods, one by one, to see which is causing the allergy or intolerance

frontal lobes
region of the brain at the front of the skull that controls selective attention

genetic
related to genes inherited from parents

hyperactive
more active than normal for the age group; 'hyper' is Greek for 'extremely'

impulsive
acting without thinking or considering the consequences

inattentive
not paying attention

intolerance
abnormal reaction to a chemical in food or the environment

methylphenidate
stimulant drug used in the treatment of ADHD and other conditions

molecules
building blocks that chemicals are made of

neuron
nerve cell that transmits nerve impulses

neurotransmitters
chemical messengers that carry information between nerve cells

noradrenaline (also norepinephrine)
chemical messenger that prompts 'fight or flight' reactions

objective
independent – not favouring either one thing or another

occupational therapist
person who uses activities to help people recover from an illness

oppositional defiant disorder (also known as conduct disorder)
uncooperative, obstructive and disobedient behaviour

PET (positron emission tomography)
brain scanning technology that records activity by detecting where radioactively tagged sugar molecules cluster

psychotherapy
treatment of a mental disorder by exploring problems with a therapist rather than with medication

sensory
relating to the sensations you receive via your eyes, ears, nose, tongue and touch

SPECT (single photon emission computed tomography)
brain scanning technology that records activity by identifying differences in blood supply to parts of the brain

stimulants
chemicals in drugs or food that stimulate the brain

synapse
gap between one nerve cell and another crossed by neurotransmitters

syndrome
group of symptoms which occur together and enable doctors to identify an illness

tenacious
holding on to something

Index